George Webb Medley, England Sheffield Junior Liberal
Association

England Under Free Trade

George Webb Medley, England Sheffield Junior Liberal Association

England Under Free Trade

ISBN/EAN: 9783744667197

Printed in Europe, USA, Canada, Australia, Japan

Cover: Foto ©ninafisch / pixelio.de

More available books at **www.hansebooks.com**

PRICE THREEPENCE.

ENGLAND UNDER FREE TRADE.

AN ADDRESS

DELIVERED TO THE SHEFFIELD JUNIOR LIBERAL ASSOCIATION, 8th NOV., 1881,

BY

GEORGE W. MEDLEY.

CASSELL, PETTER, GALPIN & CO.:

LONDON, PARIS & NEW YORK.

1881.

ENGLAND

UNDER FREE TRADE.

AN ADDRESS

DELIVERED TO THE SHEFFIELD JUNIOR LIBERAL
ASSOCIATION, 8th NOVEMBER, 1881.

BY

GEORGE W. MEDLEY.

FREE TRADE · PEACE · GOODWILL AMONG NATIONS

Cobden
Club

CASSELL, PETTER, GALPIN & CO.
LONDON, PARIS & NEW YORK.
1881.

ENGLAND UNDER FREE TRADE.

I HAVE the honour of appearing before you this evening for the purpose of delivering to you an address, which I have entitled " England under Free Trade."

Now, these are very wide terms. In their full meaning they cover a vast field of inquiry, and, if I were to attempt to traverse that field throughout, I should have to take in political, social, agricultural, commercial, artistic, literary, and other matters, which I have no intention of doing, for which there is no time, and for which I certainly have not the requisite ability. With your permission, therefore, I propose to confine myself to the one great subject indicated by my title, Free Trade, only touching on some of the others by way of argument or illustration.

In fact, our inquiry will resolve itself into a chapter of what is termed the Fair Trade Controversy.

That controversy turns, as you are aware, on the question whether the commercial policy we have adopted for the last thirty-five years has or has not contributed to the public welfare ; and, consequently, whether we ought or ought not to maintain that policy.

The question may be put shortly thus :—Is Free Trade a success or a failure ?

But, before we proceed further, let us define what we mean by the term Free Trade as just used. In the abstract, Free Trade may be defined as that state of affairs in which the nations exchange with each other their various products untrammelled by hostile and prohibitory tariffs. Protection, on the other hand, is that state of affairs in which the nations are hindered from this free exchange by tariffs imposed for that special purpose.

Well, we all know that Free Trade as thus defined does not exist. We are said to be living under Free Trade, but in a strict sense that is not so. We are living under a system in which our imports alone are free; our exports to some of the principal markets not being free. It is only as regards our imports that we enjoy perfect freedom ; and it is for this reason that the present *régime* has been called One-sided Free Trade. It will now be our task to inquire whether this has been, as regards our national welfare, a success or a failure.

Now, all parties to the controversy are agreed as to the benefits Universal Free Trade would confer on mankind. So far as I can make out, no one whose opinion is of any scientific value denies that if Free Trade were universal, it would be of infinite advantage to the human race. There are some among us, however, who maintain that partial Free Trade—such as that under which we now live—is prejudicial to the country which opens its ports to foreign productions, and beneficial to the country which, on the other hand, shuts out, as far as it can, by prohibitory duties, the commodities of other nations. And this is just the point of the discussion. Let us call to mind why it is that Universal Free Trade is so beneficial. It is because a vital and energetic principle which political economists call "Co-operation of Labour" is brought into most efficient play. Free Trade in a natural manner causes each nation to produce those commodities which are most suitable to its soil, and to the circumstances and the genius of the inhabitants of the particular region ; and to exchange the commodities thus produced for the products of other nations, who, in like manner, have their own peculiar advantages and industries. In such happy circumstances energy, invention, and enterprise are allowed full play, and, as regards wealth, there is a constant tendency, by means of more extended division of labour, and improvement of processes, towards the maximum of production at the minimum of cost. "But," as Mill says, speaking under the head of "International Trade," "the economical advantages of commerce are surpassed in importance by those of its effects, which are intellectual and moral." "Finally," a little further on he says, "commerce first taught nations to see with goodwill the wealth and prosperity of one another. Before, the patriot—unless sufficiently advanced in culture to feel the world his country—wished all countries weak, poor, and ill-governed but his own ; he now sees in their wealth and progress a direct source of wealth and progress to his own country. It is commerce which is rapidly rendering war obsolete, by strengthening and multiplying the personal interests which are in opposition to it. And it may be said without exaggeration that the great extent and rapid increase of international trade, in being the principal guarantee of the peace of the world, is the great permanent security for the uninterrupted progress of the ideas, the institutions, and the character of the human race."

As I have before remarked, all parties are agreed as to the economic advantages of Universal Free Trade, but there are some who, while admitting to the fullest the economical, or £ s. d. side of the Free Trade doctrine, maintain that it has also a political side. They admit that Free Trade tends to achieve the maximum of production at the minimum of cost, but they say that there are other things to be considered besides the accumulation of the greatest possible amount of wealth. One of the things to be considered, they say, is the necessity of educating a community in such arts and manufactures as its resources are naturally fitted for, but of which, except for Protection, it would remain ignorant. And another thing to be considered, they say, is this :—that so long as human nature is what it is, and nations are liable to go to war, it is not only prudent and statesmanlike, but absolutely necessary, in view of such a contingency, to endeavour to render their country as far as possible independent of the foreigner. And thus, according to this school, the doctrine of Protection may be reasonably maintained.

Now, I have two remarks to make concerning this doctrine. As regards the education of a people in an industrial art by means of Protection, it may safely be conceded that if the protection be withdrawn when the lesson is learnt, no great harm would be done, and a great benefit might be conferred. But, we know from experience that this is most unlikely to happen ; and that when once Protection has been admitted into a commercial system it becomes the most difficult thing in the world to get rid of it. Then, with regard to the contingency of war, how different are the views of the school of which I speak from those held by that association to which I have the honour to belong—the Cobden Club ! While the school referred to seems to be always .contemplating and preparing for the contingency of war by means of hostile tariffs, we are striving might and main to render war impossible, by preaching our commercial gospel of peace !

As you are all aware, Great Britain stands alone among the nations as a free-trading country. It is natural to inquire how this is the case, how it is that people, acute, thoughtful, and intelligent, as, for instance, the French, the Germans, and the Americans, cling to the doctrines of Protection, while we alone adhere to those of Free Trade ? A full answer to that question, gentlemen, would occupy more time than we have at command this evening. I must content myself with just indicating the direction in which I believe the causes of this phenomenon are to be traced. I cannot help thinking that most of the evil is to be laid to the account of wars. Their cost necessitates the imposition of heavy taxation. The persons who impose that taxation are for the most part ignorant of political economy. They take the first impost that occurs to them, and they lay it on the people they misgovern. They know nothing of the possible consequences, in an economic point of view, of what they do. One of these consequences is the creation of interests which would never have existed but for this cause, which grow up, and which gradually acquire sufficient influence and power to render it extremely difficult to get rid of them. This difficulty I hold to be the great economic problem of the immediate future.

At the present moment we may see these causes in operation in France, Germany, and the United States ; what is taking place there affording apt illustrations. We ourselves have suffered in times past from these causes, but thirty-five years ago, we embraced Free Trade, and during that period we have been gradually emancipating ourselves from their baneful influence. The countries I have named, however, still cling to Protection, and there seems to be no immediate probability of their changing their creed. If I be asked—Is this not an astonishing fact? I should answer—Not at all. England has been ahead of the rest or the world in other things before now. We had our revolu tion, and settled matters with our king, a hundred years before France did ; in the matter of the abolition of slavery we were thirty-five years before the Americans ; while as to Germany, the Cæsarism, the militarism, the despotism which reign there, and which impoverish her, place her in some respects a hundred years behind us in the march or civilisation.

The ground is now sufficiently cleared, I trust, for us to take a survey of our position under what is called our one-sided Free Trade. The first thing to which I shall call your attention is the Board of Trade returns, which, as you know, give the particulars of our trade with the rest of the world under the heads of Imports and Exports. The totals of these, as you are aware, have been growing, with slight interruptions, ever larger and larger year by year, until last year the sum total of our foreign trade amounted to the stupendous figure of 697 millions, which figure seems likely to be eclipsed by that of the year which is now drawing to its close. Of this trade our imports amounted to 411 millions, and our exports to 286 millions, leaving an excess of imports of 125 millions. Now, let me remind you that it is in regard to this excess of imports over exports that the Fair Trade battle most hotly rages. The Fair Traders maintain that this excess of 125 millions is the measure of our national loss for 1880; while the Free Trader ridicules this view, and maintains, on the contrary, that it may more justly be considered a measure of our national gain.

In a little pamphlet call " The Reciprocity Craze," which I had the honour of writing for the Cobden Club, I made the assertion that this question of imports and exports constituted the *pons asinorum*, or "asses' bridge" of the Fair Trade controversy. Gentlemen, I reiterate that assertion, and, with your permission, we will endeavour to pass over this bridge, hand in hand, as it were.

The Fair Traders say something like this :—John Bull buys of the foreigner 411 million pounds' worth of goods, and sells him only 286 million pounds' worth, and they deduce from this that there is a balance of trade against him of 125 millions, which is a loss to him, by which he is so much the poorer ; and that he is thus losing his wealth to the benefit of the foreigner, who has the best of the trade. And they maintain further that John Bull is getting poorer and poorer ; that if the system goes on it must end in his ruin ; and that all this is the genuine and unavoidable outcome of one-sided Free Trade. The Free Trader, as I have said, ridicules this view. He asks, in the first place, why the bare fact of our importing more than we export should be held to involve a loss—seeing that to get in more than one gives out appears to ordinary minds the only way of realising a profit.

And for the following reasons :—

In my pamphlet I asked this question—If a merchant export £100 worth of goods, and in exchange for them, imports goods worth only £100, how can he do otherwise than make a dead loss under the heads of freight, insurance, interest, and profits? Let us suppose the goods cost him £100 at Liverpool. He exports them to some foreign country, and, of course, has to pay freight and insurance. Let us say this comes to 10 per cent. On arrival at the foreign market the goods must therefore be worth £110. They must be sold, of course, and let us suppose the proceeds re-invested in goods for importation here. Again comes in the charge for freight, another 10 per cent., which, added to the £110, makes the goods worth £121 on arrival at our ports, independently of interest on the money used, and what our merchant may lay on as profit.

And so the £100 of exports comes back as £121, at least, of imports, and must do so as long as trade is carried on.

In further illustration, let me quote from Mr. J. K. Cross's speech in the House on the 12th of August. He says, " £1,000 will buy 2,000 tons of coal free on board at Cardiff; the freight of this coal to San Francisco will be £1,500; the amount realised for it in San Francisco will be £2,500, which sum, invested in wheat, will purchase 2,000 quarters. The conveyance of this wheat to Liverpool will cost £1,500, and it will require to be sold at £4,000 in Liverpool to cover cost and expenses. In the import tables there will be an entry of £4,000 of wheat; in the export tables there will be an entry of £1,000 coal; the one exchanges for the other."

The Fair Trader, however, regardless of all such considerations, persists in asserting that every year we *buy* of the foreigner more than we *sell* him. The fallacy under which he labours arises, of course, from the use of the terms *buy—sell*. The Free Trader, with a more just appreciation of what takes place, discards these terms in the sense thus implied, and rightly says :—So far as commodities are concerned, we got in 411 millions of them, and gave out only 286 millions, and if that were all to be considered, it seems to be a mighty fine business.

But, there are a great many things to be considered, as we shall soon see. One great thing to be considered is, whether John Bull at the end of each year owes anything to anybody for his excess of imports. Everything turns upon this; so we will at once proceed to put the matter to the test. Now, in order to assist us in the investigation, let me lay down this proposition, which I consider an axiom :—That in international commerce there are three, and only three, modes of squaring accounts—namely, by commodities, bullion, or securities; in other words, that between nation and nation, debts can only be settled and liquidated in some one or more of these three modes. Let us apply this axiom to the facts of our commerce as recorded in our official returns. I will first take the figures of the last eleven years, because, as they comprise the latest periods of inflation and depression of trade, they are calculated to give us a correct notion as to what has been going on. Now, what do these records say as to commodities? I find that during this period our imports in round numbers were 4,016 millions, and our exports 3,022 millions, leaving an excess of imports of 994 millions—994 millions ! How in the name of fortune, one is inclined to ask, was this excess settled for ? How much gold and silver went out of the country to pay for these 994 millions of commodities ? Let us see. Again we turn to the records, and we find that during the period in question our imports of the precious metals were in round numbers 341 millions, and our exports 306 millions, leaving in our hands 35 millions. It actually turns out, therefore, that we have not only got these commodities, but have, in addition, pocketed this large sum on balance, notwithstanding the fight for gold which has been going on in the world for currency purposes. But surely, some one will say, it cannot be possible for us to have got in all these goods, and all this cash, without parting with our securities ? We shall see. We have no Board of Trade returns for our foreign loan and investments account, so we must be content with an approximate estimate. You have all heard of foreign loans, many good, some bad. Well, during these eleven years, probably 500 millions of these were floated in London. Let us say we took one half of them, that is 250 millions. Then, for purchases of American and other securities, and for investments in all sorts of foreign industrial enterprises, and for commercial advances, let us put down a balance of 100 millions. These two amounts give us a total of 350 millions, for which John Bull has made the world his debtor during these eleven years. We thus see that what with the goods, cash, and securities, John Bull, who is supposed all this while to have been going to the dogs, has managed to appropriate on balance no less a sum than 1,380 millions sterling. I think you will admit that this is not a bad result for a nation which is said to have been going to ruin fast during the last few years. The idea of ruin is ridiculous, farcical ! Mark, there is no possible escape from the conclusion. I have shown that as a nation we, in this series of years, have managed to acquire on balance all these three things—commodities, bullion, and securities ; and that, as there is no other mode of settling international accounts but by means of one or other of these three, the proof I give amounts to mathematical demonstration.

A similar result is found whether we take ten, or twenty, or any series of years during the Free Trade epoch. I have before me the figures for the last twenty-seven years, that is, going back to 1854, and from them I find that in those twenty-seven years, our excess of commodities imported was 1,742 millions, our excess of bullion imported was 131 millions, and our excess of securities imported was 600 millions, making a grand total of 2,473 millions as profit on our last twenty-seven years' foreign trade.

There can be no question, therefore, that as a nation we have become richer and richer. But, while I assert and prove this, I do not mean to assert that there has been at all times, and among all classes, an equal distribution of the wealth acquired. That is another and a totally different question. During the American Civil War, for instance, when there was a cotton famine, our manufacturing interests suffered great losses and privations. Then, during the last few years, the agricultural interest, and the interests which depend on it, have suffered most severely. I do not for one moment deny that some of our interests have suffered. With those sufferings I warmly sympathise, but while I acknowledge them, and condole respecting them, I cannot be driven from the position I take up that the nation, as a whole, is prosperous, the mathematical proof of this being found in the fact that year by year, on the whole, we get in on balance commodities, bullion, and securities.

Let me illustrate this by what is said of space, namely, that it has three, and only three, dimensions—length, breadth, and thickness. Now, no one has ever seriously propounded the existence of a fourth dimension, and I say that, until the existence of this fourth dimension has been proved, and until the existence of a fourth mode of settling international transactions has been discovered—so long as we get in on balance, in a series of years, the three things I have named—we may depend upon it we are getting richer and not poorer as regards our foreign commerce.

From what you have heard you will be able easily to understand how mistakes and fallacies are sure to crop up by doing what the Fair Traders do with the bare figures of trade returns, that is to say, by looking at them without taking into account, or consideration, a number of other facts and circumstances without which they are not only useless, but are absolutely misleading and mischievous. No one can get anything like a correct notion of what is going on between nation and nation until he has taken such matters as the following into account :—He must not only look at the bare figures of imports and exports, he must know the rules by which they are computed ; and the rules differ in different countries. He must find out whether country A is lending capital to or buying the securities of country B, or whether the contrary is taking place ; or whether A is paying off debt, or paying interest on loans and other securities to B ; or whether B is doing all that to A. And, further, he must take into account the great ocean-carrying trade, and allow for freights and insurance ; and he must see who provides the capital for this international trade, and whose merchants and bankers do the business, and thus earn the profits, and the commissions; and he must also take into account such matters as payments for war indemnities, alterations of currency, and the complications arising out of fluctuations of prices, and out of changes in the standard of value. I say, that in order to obtain a perfectly accurate knowledge of what a nation is doing, the inquirer must know, and properly work in, all these various factors. But, as besides the figures in the trade returns we have no official figures, we can only roughly estimate other factors from such sources as are available, and arrive as nearly as we can at a correct conclusion.

Well now, let me ask, did you ever know or hear of a Fair Trader doing anything of that kind ? I venture to say there is not one of them who, until lately, has had the faintest notion of what is required, and that the faint notion, such as it is, which they possess, has been instilled into them by their opponents during this discussion.

Bearing in mind these considerations, let us now examine some of the facts and arguments relied on by our friends the Fair Traders.

One of the facts relied on, is that our markets are flooded by foreign goods, to the detriment of the native workman ; and the argument founded on this supposed fact is, that we ought to tax foreign manufactures, so that we may, by this means, either reduce these importations, and so increase our corresponding home productions, or, on the other hand, induce or compel foreign nations to reduce their high tariffs, and thus enable us to export more to them. Let us first see how the fact stands as regards the flooding of our markets. Our exports of manufactured goods amount to between 200 and 220 millions, and our imports to 45 millions. For every pounds' worth, therefore, that we import, we export nearly five pounds' worth, and this is what is called flooding our markets. The truth is, that the flooding is the other way, that Protectionist nations are straining every nerve to keep out our productions, and are utterly unable to do so. So much for the fact relied on. Let us see how their argument works respecting the 45 millions of manufactures which we import—one-ninth only of our whole importation—the other eight-ninths being food and raw materials, which we get from all nations put together. We are told that we ought to tax, and possibly keep out, most of these 45 millions. But the consequences of doing so might be very awkward for us.

Foreigners might do one of three things. 1. They might turn Free Traders in consequence of our action. 2. They might retaliate by further taxing our exports to them. 3. They might submit to our imposts, and do the best they could in the circumstances. As to their turning Free Traders, I cannot for a moment believe that at all likely to happen in consequence of our action. Their policy drifts more and more towards Protection, and is intended, apparently, not so much to extend exports as to restrict imports, and they most likely would retaliate on us by a war of tariffs, which would be most damaging to us, seeing that they have a field of taxation of our exports of 200 to 220 millions, while we could tax them on only 45 millions. Surely that is not a pleasant contingency to contemplate ! Then comes the third alternative, of their submitting to our imposts, and selling us as much as we should be able to take under the circumstances. And what would be the circumstances? Prices would of course be raised, and the consumer of these foreign goods would either buy less of them, or he would have to pay more for what he wants of them. In the first case, production on the part of the foreigner is checked, and he either gives up his manufacture, and thus loses his purchasing power in the world's markets, and you lose him as a customer—directly or indirectly, as I shall show you presently; or else, being baffled in your market, he turns his attention to neutral markets, competes with and injures you there, and perhaps drives you out of them. Anyhow, you impoverish both yourself and him. In the second case, where our home consumer consents to pay more for the article he wants, it is clear that, whatever the increased price may be, by so much is he directly impoverished—by so much is he less able to buy other commodities. There is less production; less demand for goods, and for labour; less trade; less shipping; less everything which contributes to make up the moral and material well-being of mankind.

And now let me explain practically what I meant when I spoke just now about our losing a customer directly or indirectly. Let us take French silks and French wines. It is a favourite idea with Fair Traders to tax these productions, because, as they urge, France does not buy of us anything like what she sells to us, and they arrive at the conclusion from this bare fact, that this is a state of things favourable to French commerce and detrimental to English commerce, in fine, a one-sided Free Trade extremely hurtful to us. Now, I wish particularly to draw your attention to this view of theirs, because in it is wrapped up one of the grossest fallacies of our opponents. This is what they overlook :—

By buying silks and wines of France, we give her so much purchasing power in the world's markets, a power which, as her trade returns show—she is a large importer upon balance—she fully exercises. Well, if she spends the money she receives from you in those products of foreign

countries which she requires, as we know she does, she
thereby, in turn, confers on those countries a corresponding
purchasing power, and they, in their turn, lay out the money
so received among other nations, and, as we are the principal
manufacturers, we get the principal share in the business.

So that by this indirect and roundabout way, everything
England buys of France, even in the way of wines and silks,
enables England to sell her products to other nations, and
thus to pay for those silks and wines; England all the while,
as the great carrying and trading nation, getting a tremen-
dous pull by way of freights, insurance, and commissions,
all of which are created by this all-round trade.

What were the figures of our trade with France last year ?

I see that our imports from her were about 42 millions,
while our exports to her were only about 15½ millions ;
leaving, apparently, a balance against us of about 26½ millions. Did we pay away any cash for this ? Not a bit of
it. Instead of paying anything, we received from France
last year in gold and silver no less a sum than £3,411,000.
You are now, however, in a position not to be in the least
astonished at what appears at first sight an absurd result. It
would appear, if we only looked at the Board of Trade
returns, and at nothing else, that last year France made
this country a present of 26½ millions of goods, and 3½ millions of money ! But we know that this is impossible, and
that France, in some shape or other, has received full value,
and it affords a good illustration of the necessity which
exists for taking other things into account besides the bare
figures of trade returns. I do wish our friends the Fair
Traders would consider fairly and honestly this crucial
example of France, and make their theory of the so-called
adverse English balance of trade square with the facts as
they stand. Whether they recognise the necessity or not,
they are bound to show how we settled accounts with
France last year, a country from which, in the course of a
twelvemonth, we got in money and in goods, and apparently
for nothing, no less a sum than 30 millions sterling ! Of
course, gentlemen, you and I know now how it was done,
and in time perhaps the more intelligent of our Fair Traders

will also find out. When they find it out, however, their
occupation will be gone. And now I will tell them something which they may perhaps not know, and which may
console them from their point of view. It is this : that the
balance in favour of France in 1880 was not as large as it
appears, as Mr. Chamberlain pointed out in his speech on
the French treaty. He tells us, " The returns of the Board
of Trade must be taken with qualifications, and applied
with knowledge. The figures for the French imports must
be reduced by what is re-exported to the United States and
our Colonies ; and for those textiles of different kinds which
come from Switzerland through France, and which are inex-
tricably mixed up with our French imports. With regard to
our exports, on the other hand, they have to be increased
by the amounts due for yarns intended for French manufactures in the Vosges, which go by way of Antwerp, and
which, therefore, do not appear in the exports to France."
The consequence is, that the balance against us is not 26½
millions, but something considerably less, and this will probably console our Fair Trade friends. We must not, however, reduce this balance too much, for if we do, we shall
demolish entirely that grievance of theirs about France ;
and from their point of view that would be a great calamity !

But I have not done yet by a long way with our friends.
I mean to pursue to the bitter end their argument as to
taxing foreign manufactures.

The ruling idea of the Fair Trader is, apparently, to ac-
complish one of two things. If the foreigner taxes our
manufactures, we are to tax his ; if he admits our goods
free, we are to admit his goods free. He contends that if
we are compelled, in the first case, to keep out foreign
goods, our workmen will step into the place thus left vacant,
and supply our home market with these or similar goods.
But, there are goods with which we cannot be supplied at
home owing to disabilities of soil and climate, to say nothing of race, but which it is of actual necessity, or prime
convenience, for us to obtain. After what I have said, it
must be clear that by taxing these, so far from helping the
British workman, we should only impoverish him. There

are other commodities, however, which the Fair Trader thinks would be supplied by the home workman instead of the foreigner. But, to be of any advantage to the British manufacturer, the British workman, and the British consumer, the following impossible state of things must occur. In addition to the goods which we now make for the foreigner, we must be ready to supply our home market with much of which the foreigner now supplies us, but of which we now are to cut him out. He is to sit down quietly under this, and buy of you just as much as he did before, although you have taken away so much of his purchasing power by cutting him out! At present, the foreigner makes certain goods better and cheaper than we can. When he is cut out, our consumers will consent, cheerfully as a matter of course, to pay higher prices for these same goods! Then, on account of the new home business which is to spring up, there is to be no fresh capital required, no fresh plant, no additional workers, or, if there are, there is to be no increased cost in these respects, there is to be no change in any respect whatever, except that our manufacturers will have cut out the foreigner and got the home market in addition to the foreign market!

But, gentlemen, this is all most absurd, and I am sure I need say nothing more respecting it. I would rather proceed to inquire how it is our own people cannot supply us with certain things which now come to us from abroad ; for instance, French silks and French woollens. The simple fact is, of course, that from a variety of causes our manufacturers and workmen either cannot, or will not, supply us with these things. Whatever be the cause, I am not here tonight to point out the remedy, but, whatever that may ultimately turn out to be, no Free Trader will allow that it is to be found in taxing the foreign product. If, for instance, foreign silks and foreign woollens were to be driven out of this country by hostile tariffs, it is certain that, over and above the actual loss to us as traders, which, as I have shown, would be involved by these trades being killed, our consumers, that is, the bulk of this nation, would be driven to take up with fabrics of a kind and quality which they do not want. There is not much fear of such an eventuality, however, for I do not believe the people of this country would put up with such intolerable tyranny.

As you know, complaints have been heard of the woollen manufactures of Bradford having passed away to their French rivals. But what are the facts? As I gather them, they stand thus. We find that British alpaca or lustre has been superseded by French merino. Some years ago alpaca was in high favour. Now it is neglected, and the soft woollen worsteds of France have superseded it. How was this? As I read it, it was because, when alpaca was formerly made of pure fine lustrous wools only, it was in favour; but when manufacturers, aiming at cheap production and high profits, mixed the new wool with cotton, they produced nothing but a shoddy, which soon lost favour. Our French competitors, it appears, saw their opportunity; they bought their wools in our own market in London, they took it to France, adopted for it new machinery, and every process which promised improvement, sought for and found new dyes, inventing soft half-tints and subdued shades of colour, and then brought it back to us made up into those fabrics which are now so much in vogue, and which are known by the name of French merinos and cashmeres. Now, I wish to ask whether this is creditable to us as manufacturers? There can be no question that, from some cause or other, our manufacturers have allowed the French to steal a march on them. Let them meet the modern demand by doing as the French have done; let them adapt their machinery, and study new processes, and, depend upon it, we shall then hear very little about French competition in this department.

Now, having thus disposed of the Fair Trader's argument for taxing foreign manufactures, let me say a few words respecting his assertion that our excess of imports is to be considered the measure of our national loss. We now, on the average, import more than we export considerably over 100 millions' worth of commodities annually. We Free Traders say that instead of its being a loss to us, it is a profit to us, and that if we did not get in this excess of value we should be doing a very bad business indeed. I want to know, in the first place, why the shipowners of Great Britain, who possess one-half of the world's effective ocean tonnage, are not to receive what is due to them for the freights they carry, and if so, how they are to be paid? I want to know, in the second place, why those among us who hold foreign bonds, shares, and investments of every kind, are not to be paid the interest which is due to them, and if so, now they are to be paid? I want to know, in the third place, why our shipbuilders, who last year built 90 iron, and 160 wooden ships for the foreigner, are not to receive the price of those ships, and if so, how they are to be paid? I want to know, in the fourth place, why our merchants and bankers, who advance the capital by which our 700 millions of foreign commerce is put in motion, are not to receive the interest on their capital, and if so, how they are to be paid? And in the fifth place, I want to know if our merchants and brokers, who carry on this 700 millions of foreign trade, are to earn any commission thereon, and if so, how they are to be paid?

There are other items which might be brought into the account, but they are sufficient for my purpose; let us try and roughly estimate them. I cannot put down the gross receipts of our ocean carrying trade at less than 45 millions. With regard to the interest on our foreign investments, they are variously estimated by the best authorities at from 55 to 60 millions. I will take the smaller figure. Then the price of those 250 ships we sold last year cannot, at a moderate computation, be put down at less than 1½ million. Then, as to interest on capital, let us take 100 millions as constantly employed in moving our 700 millions of commerce, and say five per cent., this gives us 5 millions; and lastly, what are we to put down by way of commissions? 2½ per cent. on 700 millions give us 17½ millions. Let us now add up.

Shipping receipts	...	...	...	£45,000,000
Interest on investments	...	...	...	55,000,000
250 ships sold	...	...	...	1,500,000
Interest on capital	...	...	...	5,000,000
Merchants' commissions		...	...	17,500,000
				£124,000,000

From this sum, however, must be deducted what we may have to pay the foreigner on so much of our foreign commerce as he carries for us, and for the balance between what we have to pay him, and what we have to receive from him, in respect of supplies, port dues, &c., and if for these items we take off, roughly, 14 millions, there remains 110 millions to receive from the foreigner annually by way of interest on loans, and for work and labour done for him. In other words, before we have to send away a pound's worth of goods with the view of getting a pound's worth in exchange, we have to receive in some shape or other from the foreigner no less a sum annually than 110 millions sterling. In the name of political economy and common sense, how can this be a bad thing for this country?

Anyhow, and after making all possible deductions, you must see that we can import over 100 millions worth of commodities without trenching on our capital, and that is the great point. But, it may be asked, why do we take goods and not cash?

The answer to that is, that in some years we take part goods, and part cash, some years all goods, never all cash. To be paid entirely in cash is about the last thing we should want, but if we did want it, we could not get it; 100 millions loose cash in the world does not exist.

But let us suppose for a moment that we could get cash by some impossible process. What should we do with it? We could not eat it. We should not want to pile it up in vaults We should have to send it abroad again in exchange for commodities, and, if in the end you have to do that, you may as well take commodities at once, and so save the expense and loss of two voyages of your cash. The fact is, that it is only in commodities that one nation can discharge the bulk of its debts to another nation, and that if the world owes us money, and makes us its carrier and its general merchant, we *must* take payment in commodities. And thus you see, at a stroke we get rid of that bugbear to some people, the thing commonly called the Balance of Trade, and which, as commonly understood, is a fallacious and misleading expression.

There is one country which at the present moment stands in marked contrast to us as regards the balance of her imports and exports. I mean the United States. She of late years has been a large exporter on balance, and our Fair Traders have often pointed to this excess of exports as a proof of her prosperity, and of the virtues of her Protective system. When, however, we call to mind the fact that while we are a lending nation, with an excess of capital, and do more than half the ocean carrying trade of the world, and that the United States are a borrowing nation, requiring capital, and ready to pay for the use of it ; and that owing to her Protectionist policy foreigners carry more than 80 per cent. of her foreign commerce ; it is easy to see that, other things being equal, while we have to import on balance, she has to export. Now, it is impossible to estimate with any approach to accuracy what the States have to send abroad each year by way of interest on their indebtedness, and for freight, and for other things. I cannot put it down at less than 20 millions, and it is most likely a great deal more, probably nearer 40 millions. Whatever the amount may be, however, it has to be allowed the foreigner in account, and, therefore, any argument in favour of Protection, and against Free Trade, built up out of the bare figures of her trade returns, and without regard to the considerations to which I have called your attention, must necessarily be most fallacious.

If we turn to France, we shall find in her trade returns a curious exemplification of the truth of the principles on which I am insisting. As you are aware, the Franco-German war broke out in 1870 and closed in 1871. Well, just before that war, that is in 1869 and 1870, her imports and exports, according to Martin's "Statesman's Year Book," balanced each other almost exactly. You also know that in 1871 France had to pay an indemnity of 200 millions to Germany, and that she appealed abroad for a large loan to aid her to pay that indemnity. Well, in 1871 she imported on balance 21 millions. In 1872, however, and during the three following years she exported on balance 39 millions. How is this to be accounted for? By simply recalling to mind what everybody knows, that France was during those four years repaying what she had borrowed abroad ; and that at the end of 1875 she had probably repaid the bulk of it, and had recovered from the terrible losses she had incurred.   What are her trade figures since then ?

In 1876 her excess imports were	...	...	£16,500,000
In 1877	,,	,,	...	...	10,800,000
In 1878	,,	,,	...	...	43,600,000
In 1879	,,	,,	...	...	57,200,000
In 1880	,,	,,	...	...	63,000,000

and I see by a paragraph in the *Times* of the 16th September that her excess imports for the first eight months of 1881 amount to 1,097 millions of francs, or 43 millions sterling, so that Protectionist France, according to our Fair Trade friends, must be going down-hill rapidly along with Free-Trading England, for she has been rapidly and unprecedentedly increasing her excess of imports ! And now I ask Fair Traders how they reconcile these trade figures of France with their theories ?

The trade figures of Germany tell the same story. While she was receiving the French indemnity she was a large importer on balance.   When this operation was completed, this excess of imports began to diminish.   If we take 1869 and 1880, I find in "Mulhall" that while in 1869 that excess was 12 millions, in 1880 it was only 6 millions.   This is anything but a reassuring commercial sign for her.   Indeed, when we couple this fact with others which crop up, such as, for instance, the falling off of savings' bank deposits in Saxony, the increase of emigration, the increased cost of living, the decreasing earnings per head of her population, we cannot be surprised when we hear that protests against her fiscal system have been made by an overwhelming majority of her Chambers of Commerce, and that in the late elections a majority has been returned pledged to oppose the Protectionist policy of Prince Bismarck.   The fact is, that the vaunted system of Protection has utterly broken down in Germany, and that, as she is the poorest of our rivals, and consequently, the weakest financially, she is the first to show the disastrous effects of the policy she has so unwisely chosen. That this is so, may be gathered also from this little fact, that our Fair Trading friends no longer allude to Germany. "*Oh, no ! we never mention her.*"

Now, gentlemen, let us take a comparative survey of ourselves, and our great rivals, France, Germany, and the United States.

Let us first take population. In 1871 the United Kingdom numbered 31,500,000; and in 1881, 34,800,000; an increase in 10 years of 3,300,000. As to France, the population in 1872, after the cession of Alsace and Lorraine, was 36,100,000, and this year it is probably 38,000,000, not more ; an increase in 9 years of 1,900,000. As regards Germany, the population in 1871 was 41,000,000, in 1875 it was 42,700,000, and in 1881 it is probably 45,000,000, an increase in 10 years of 4,000,000. As regards the United States, in 1870 their population was 38,550,000, and in 1880 it was 50,150,000, an increase during these 10 years of 11,600,000.

The percentage of increase is thus :—

For the United Kingdom	10·0
France...	5·3
Germany	9·7
United States	30·0

You thus see that the United States lead the way in this respect. The conditions which exist there, and which cause this enormous increase, are so well known and understood that I need not refer to them further. And you will notice that France is far behind ourselves and Germany, a fact which gives rise to many considerations, into which it is impossible to enter now. Great Britain and Germany have progressed very evenly during this period ; whether they will do so during the next ten years, remains to be seen. The consolidation of the Empire drew many into Germany, but the cost of that Empire becomes more and more onerous, and there are signs that the tide of emigration is rising. Anyhow, as regards population, we stand well in comparison with the older States.

Now, let us consider some or the facts bearing on the economic condition of these four great nations. I find on referring to Mulhall's "Balance-sheet of the World, 1870—1880," that in a table of the world's industries, under the heads of commerce, manufactures, mining, agriculture, carrying and banking, he gives us the following totals :—

	1870. Millions.		Per Head. £ s. d.		1880. Millions.		Per Head. £ s. d.
Great Britain	... 1,687	...	53 13 0	...	2,024	...	58 11 0
France ...	... 1,181	...	31 0 0	...	1,325	...	35 12 0
Germany ...	... 1,002	...	26 7 0	...	1,269	...	28 1 0
United States	... 1,479	...	38 9 0	...	2,004	...	40 1 0

Taking man for man, therefore, we are far ahead of the world in industry, and, instead of going back, are actually improving our position.

Now let us see what Mulhall says of the earnings of the nations free of taxes per head of population :—

	1870.	1880.
Great Britain ...	... £26 17 1 ...	... £29 10 7
France ...	... 17 12 2 ...	... 18 12 5
Germany ...	... 16 16 6 ...	... 16 9 8
United States ...	... 23 17 10 ...	... 25 5 0

Man for man we thus, as regards our earnings, not only stand at the head of the list, but have gained on our competitors.

Let us now look at what is said under the head of manufactures :—

MANUFACTURES :—TEXTILES, HARDWARE, SUNDRIES.

	1870. Millions.		Per Head. £ s. d.		1880. Millions.		Per Head £ s. d
Great Britain...	... 642	...	20 8 0	...	758	...	22 0 0
France ...	... 439	...	11 11 0	...	485	...	13 2 0
Germany ...	... 341	...	9 0 0	...	427	...	9 9 0
United States	... 682	...	17 14 0	...	888	...	17 15 0

Once more we see that we not only stand at the head of the list, but are far ahead of Germany and the United States, France making the best show against us.

Let us now examine the figures concerning ocean shipping. What is shown is the effective tonnage, arrived at by multiplying steam tonnage by 5 in order to get a common denominator :—

	1869. Tons.	1879. Tons.
Great Britain	9,520,000	16,630,000
France	1,598,000	1,960,000
Germany	1,310,000	1,950,000
United States	2,454,000	2,315,000

We thus see that while in these ten years we have increased our effective tonnage by 7 millions, the United States have lost 140,000 tons !

Gentlemen, these shipping figures are conclusive. Protectionist nations may, by *hocus pocus*, conceal the losses they internally suffer from their system, but they cannot conceal the facts which these figures show.

And lastly, let us see how it fares with us all as regards foreign commerce. Take the totals :—

	1870. £	Per Head. £ s. d.	1880. £	Per Head. £ s. d.
Great Britain	547,338,070	17 10 10	697,644,031	20 4 10
France	249,000,000	6 9 0	332,000,000	8 17 0
Germany	270,000,000	7 2 0	384,000,000	8 10 0
United States	172,000,000	4 9 0	301,000,000	6 0 0

The above figures are taken from Mulhall's "Balance-sheet of the World," as I have said, and they speak for themselves.

I will now quote from an admirably written article in the October number of the *Nineteenth Century*, written by Mr. Thomas P. Whittaker :—

"The following are the amounts of the exports of Great Britain and the United States to the five divisions of the globe for the year 1878, as given by the Americans themselves (excluding the trade between the two countries) :—

	Exports from the United States.		Exports from Great Britain.
Africa	... 4,468,040	...	... 59,503,000
Asia	... 12,519,000	...	... 226,590,000
America (excluding U.S.)	93,152,000	...	... 140,100,000
Australasia ...	... 6,771,000	...	... 104,611,000
Europe (excluding G.B.)	260,927,000	...	... 556,554,000
	$377,837,040		$1,087,358,000
Or ...	£75,567,400		£217,471,600

"Where are the United States as an exporting nation in the neutral markets of Africa, Asia, and Australasia? To those three divisions of the globe they send £4,751,000 worth of goods, while we send £78,140,800 worth! Even to the peoples of North and South America, at their very doors, our exports are one-half more than theirs, and theirs are mainly food."

Well, gentlemen, besides being Englishmen, you are Sheffield men; and having heard what I have had to say concerning our common country and her commercial position, and having, I hope, come to the conclusion that England is prospering, you are probably ready to hear what I have to say about Sheffield, and Sheffield trade in particular.

With your permission we will follow a line of inquiry similar to that taken with regard to the nation at large. We will first take population. I find that in 1871 the population was 239,946, and in 1881, 284,464, an increase of 18 per cent. Well, there is no indication of decay in these figures; but before we can form a correct idea of the progress of your town, we must look at other factors. Let us take pauperism. In 1871, your paupers numbered on the 1st of January, 7,560; in 1881, 7,126; decrease, 434. So that with 44,000 more inhabitants you have 400 less paupers! If you had kept to the same ratio as in 1871, you would have had 9,000 and not 7,126.

That, at all events, is a satisfactory indication. Let us now, from the Savings Bank returns, see how Sheffield fares in the matter of thrift. As you are aware, there are two kinds of Savings Banks, the old Trustee Banks, and the new Post Office Banks. With regard to the former, I find that in 1870 the number of accounts open was 21,533, and the deposits, £493,998 ; while in 1880 the number of accounts open was 29,254, and the deposits, £759,427 ; an increase of £265,430.

As regards the Post Office Banks, I have only the figures from 1873 to 1879. In 1873 the number of depositors was 6,639, and the amount deposited, £59,008. In 1879 the number of depositors was 7,884, and the amount deposited, £78,125. Now, we know that in 1880 there was a great accession of deposits, and we may safely reckon that on the 31st December, 1880, there was £80,000 in these banks. Taking these last eight years, therefore, of both descriptions of banks, we find that whereas in 1873 the deposits were £688,791, in 1880 they were £839,427 ; which, considering the times through which you have passed, may be considered a most satisfactory result.

We will now look at the statistics of crime :—

Year.	Population.	Convictions and Committals.
1870	235,500	2,162
1871	239,946	2,102
1880	280,000	2,075

This again is highly satisfactory.

We will now take elementary education :—

Return of the Numbers of Children attending efficient Elementary Schools, from the period at which the Sheffield School Board commenced operations to October, 1880.

Year.	Average Yearly Attendance.	No. on Rolls October.
1871	11,985	No return.
1872	14,052	ditto.
1873	18,820	35,073
1876	26,713	42,736
1879	31,522	47,422
1880	32,817	50,319

Here we see that while in 1873 there was an average attendance of 53·7 per cent. of the children on the rolls ; in 1881 that average had risen to 65·2 per cent.

Now, so far as these figures go, they indicate that materially, morally, and intellectually, Sheffield is in a far better position than she occupied ten years ago.

But, what these figures teach us is corroborated by what is to be ascertained from our Board of Trade Returns. Your town is interested in iron, steel, and all kinds of hardware. Let us compare the figures of 1870 and 1871 with those of 1879 and 1880.

Let me draw your attention in the first instance to the following table of our exports of all sorts of ironwork :—

YEAR.			TONS.			VALUE.
1870	...	...	2,825,575	...	...	24,038,090
1871	...	...	3,169,219	...	...	26,124,134
1879	...	...	2,883,484	...	...	19,417,363
1880	...	...	3,792,993	...	...	28,390,316

Great Britain, therefore, did much better in her iron and steel in 1880 than in 1879, and, as a matter of course, Sheffield participated largely in the benefit. This is shown in certain figures which I find in the *Sheffield Independent,* to which paper I am indebted for them as well as for many other valuable ones on the subject.

I see that the exports of Sheffield to America in 1877 were £450,000 ; in 1879, £560,000 ; in 1880, £1,066,000 ; and that the total for the twelve months ending 30th September, 1881, was £1,223,830, being £157,419 over the total for the twelve months ending 30th September, 1880.

The prices of 1880, however, are not equal to those of 1870, and, of course, so far as this goes, there is not so much profit, but, inasmuch as there has been a general fall in prices during this period, the difference is not all loss, and what is gained by the fall in all other products has to be set off against this loss, so that, in the end, I suspect there would not be much to complain of in this respect. I have not time now to enter into the questions arising out of the fall in prices. It is, however, a most important and interesting subject. Anyhow, the prices of 1880 are better than the prices of 1879, and the prices of 1881 are, I believe, exceeding those of 1880.

Let us now see what Sheffield is doing in 1881 in all foreign markets. We have the Board of Trade returns for September. They show that the total value of hardware and cutlery exported for that month was £340,362, against £298,069 for September, 1880; and that the total for the nine months was £2,776,380, against £2,547,267 for the corresponding nine months of 1880. So far all is satisfactory, but, before I have done with statistics, I should like to give you another view of Sheffield trade by instituting a comparison of our iron, steel, and hardware trade with France, Germany, and the United States respectively. The figures I shall quote come direct from the Board of Trade.

Those referring to the United States are printed in the Appendix to Mr. Chamberlain's speech on the French Treaty in the House on the 12th August, as published by the Cobden Club. Those which refer to France and Germany have been forwarded to me on my application.

I find that as regards France, our importations of iron and steel manufactures for 1880 amounted to £118,000, while our exports to France for the same period were of partly manufactured articles of iron, wrought and unwrought, £789,000; of manufactured articles—fire-arms, £5,000; other kinds, £3,000; hardware and cutlery, £174,000; steam-engines, £129,000; other machinery, £567,000; total £1,667,000. As regards Germany, during 1880, our exports of hardware to her were as follows :—Iron, wrought and unwrought, £1,145,000; manufactured goods— hardware and cutlery, £182,000; implements and tools, £13,000; steam-engines, £228,000; other machinery, £843,000; total £2,411,000; while as to our imports of iron and steel, on searching for this item I find literally *nil*; there is no entry whatever under this head in the paper which I hold in my hand, which I have received from the Board of Trade, and which is open to the inspection of any one !

Let us now turn to the United States. Our exports to them in 1880 were—pig-iron and old iron, £3,233,000; wrought iron, £6,814,000; machinery, £439,000; hardware and cutlery, £494,000; total, £10,980,000; while our imports from them of iron and steel manufactured goods came to £213,000.

So far, therefore, as Sheffield is concerned, we export to these three countries whom we are taught to consider our rivals, and successful rivals, these countries which are said to be flooding us with their goods, we exported, I say, to them in 1880 no less a value in iron and steel, and hardware goods, than £15,058,000, while we imported from them of like goods only £341,000.

Gentlemen, I think that we may gather from these figures that Sheffield is tolerably safe. Yet, as you know, there have been complaints that American iron, steel, and hardware are flooding our home markets. Well, this flooding, as you have seen, amounts to the stupendous figure of £213,000. It consisted probably of novelties, clever adaptations, ingenious appliances, in the way of scythes, scissors, saws, sewing machines, hay-forks, and such like trifles. Well now, as to hay-forks. I have never seen an American one, but a friend of mine told me the other day that an American hay-fork was something quite different from an English one, that it was easy and pleasant to handle, and that with it he could do twice as much work as with an English one. Now, this is not creditable to us, I think. I want to know why I am to be compelled to work with an obsolete hay-fork when I can get one so superior? Is there no enterprising Sheffield man here present who will deliver us from this flood of hay-forks? A year hence such a thing as an American hay-fork ought not to be seen in this country except as a curiosity. I do wish somebody would seize on this idea, which I freely offer him, would carry it out, and succeed with it, for then my visit to Sheffield will not have been in vain.

Well, gentlemen, I trust that by this time you have been able to form a pretty accurate notion of our condition as a nation of manufacturers, trades, and carriers, and that you can come to no other conclusion than that our position is an excellent one, and one which is principally due to Free Trade as its great efficient cause. Yet, as you know, you have been called upon, and are being called upon, to disturb this satisfactory condition of things. Two associations, one of them called the National League, and the other the National Fair Trade League, have organised themselves with the view, among other objects, of procuring an alteration in our commercial policy.

I am happy to say that as regards Free Trade, these efforts have met with but little success, and that as time rolls on there is every reason to expect they will meet with still less. As, day by day, we get over one by one our commercial troubles, and, little by little, find ourselves emerging from a long protracted depression, it will be harder and harder for the advocates of Fair Trade, *alias* Protection, to delude the people into taxing their right hands a shilling, for the slender chance of getting back sixpence with their left. That little game is just two years too late ! Had they begun their agitation two years ago, when depression was at its worst, they would have made more disciples, and have given us Free Traders much more trouble to expose their shallow sophistries. Unfortunately for them now, they hardly ever commit themselves to a statement, or venture on an argument, but the next day some most inconvenient fact turns up in the news of the day to confound them. The time they have chosen for galvanising the mummy of Protection is about the worst they could have selected. It is as if some man, undertaking to prove the extinction of the sun, were to choose as the best time for making his assertions and giving his proofs, not the midnight hour—when darkness reigns and seems to lend confirmation to his statements—but the dawn, just when the orb of day begins to brighten creation, and every moment brings with it an accession of light and heat, and serves to prove him either a cunning knave or the victim of a craze.

And now, by way of contrast to our present condition under Free Trade—One-sided Free Trade—let us for a few moments take a glance back to that state of things which existed in the days of Protection, and to which we should

most assuredly revert, were we to follow the counsels of our
friends the Fair Traders.   From what they tell us, one would
suppose that such things as agricultural and commercial
depression were unknown in those happy days, and that
they only came into being with the advent of Free Trade in
1846.   I will now quote to you, by way of illustration, a few
passages from the article in the October number of the *Nineteenth Century*, entitled "The Proposals of the Fair Trade
League," from the pen of Mr. T. P. Whittaker, to which I
have already referred.

"In 1816 the poor rates at Hinckley, Leicester, were 52s.
in the pound.

"It was stated in the House of Commons in 1817 that at
Langdon in Dorsetshire, a parish containing 575 inhabitants,
409 were receiving relief.   And at Ely three-fourths of the
people were in receipt of relief.

"In 1817 wheat averaged 94s. 9d. a quarter.   In 1822
wheat fell to 43s. 4d. a quarter.   In 1819, 1820, and 1822,
agriculture was in a state of universal distress, bordering on
bankruptcy, and petitions for relief were presented to Parlia-
ment from all parts of the country.   In 1822 a Parliamentary
Committee was appointed to inquire into the cause of the
distress.   Farmers were ruined by thousands.   One news-
paper in Norwich advertised 120 sales of stock in one day.
This was when the Corn Laws were in full force, and the price
fixed by law for importing corn was 80s. a quarter.

"Again, ten years later, agricultural distress was great.
The Marquis of Stafford used to take his rents in the value
of corn, and in 1827 he abated 30 per cent., and in 1828, 26
per cent.   In 1829, the workhouses in some parts of the
country were so crowded, that at times four, five, or six people
had to sleep in one bed.

"In 1829, families in Yorkshire were reduced to live on
bran, and in Huddersfield 13,226 were reduced to semi-
starvation.

"Sir Richard Phillips, in his "Facts" (published 1832),
says :—' The dear corn years, from 1809 to 1818, swelled the
list of crimes from 5,350 in 1809 to 14,254 in 1818.   In
1839 wheat went up to 70s. 8d. a quarter, and averaged 67s.

from then to 1841, and the distress in manufacturing districts was heartrending.'

"In 1839-42 Stockport was almost desolate, one-half of the factories were shut up ; 3,000 dwellings were unoccupied, artizans were breaking stones on the roads, and the poor rate was 10s. in the pound.

"In Bolton, in 1842, the Poor Protection Society had 6,995 applicants for relief, whose earnings only averaged 13d. per head ; 5,305 persons were visited, and they had only 466 blankets amongst them, or about one blanket to every eleven persons.

"In one district in Manchester it was found that there were 2,000 families without a bed. In Glasgow, in 1842, 12,000 people were on the relief funds.

"In Accrington, out of a population of 9,000 people, only 100 were fully employed.

"In 1842, the reports of the factory inspectors showed that 10 per cent. of the cotton mills and 12 per cent. of all the woollen mills of Lancashire and Yorkshire were standing idle, and that of the rest only one-fourth were working full time."

And, in further illustration, I will quote from a speech made in the House of Commons by Cobden, in answer to Sir Robert Peel, as set out in Morley's " Life " of the great Free Trade Apostle :—

"Cobden, in answer to Sir Robert Peel, out of the fulness of his knowledge, showed that the stocking frames of Nottingham were as idle as the looms of Stockport, that the glass-cutters of Stourbridge and the glovers of Yeovil were undergoing the same privation as the potters of Stoke and the miners of Staffordshire, where 25,000 men were destitute of employment. He knew of a place where 100 wedding-rings had been pawned in a single week to provide bread, and of another place where men and women subsisted on boiled nettles, and dug up the decayed carcase of a cow rather than perish of hunger."

Well, gentlemen, it is only necessary to compare the state of affairs when these horrors took place, with that which now exists, to see that in wealth, morals, and intelli-

gence, we have made a prodigious advance during the last
forty years. In 1841, under Protection, the United Kingdom numbered 26¾ millions ; in 1881, under Free Trade,
we number 34¼ millions. In 1881, under Free Trade, there
is not a man, woman, or child of these 34¾ millions—8 millions more than existed under Protection—who is not better
off than he or she would have been under the old starvation
laws. There is no class of labourers that I know of who
do not command higher money wages now than they could
then ; and who with these wages cannot command more of
the necessaries, the conveniences, and the luxuries of life
than they could then, and who are thus enabled to get the
utmost possible return for their labour. If it be not presump-
tuous in me to give a word of advice to our artizans and
labourers, I would take the opportunity to say this : Endeavour,
if possible, to master some of the first principles of Political
Economy. Acquaint yourselves, for instance, with the meaning of the word Capital. Recognise in Capital that portion
of wealth which is devoted to reproductive purposes, and that,
as one of its chief purposes is the payment of wages, it should
be treated as a friend, to be cultivated and encouraged, not
as an enemy, to be plundered or destroyed. These things,
however, are now, I am happy to say, better understood
than they were. Trades Unions and Co-operative Companies
are doing good service in the way of education respecting
them, and are, I trust, preparing the way for the abolition
of those disgraces to civilisation, those trade wars called
strikes and lock-outs, which are as barbarous in their way
as international war is in its way, and are much more
nexcusable.

And, now, let me in conclusion say this : I hold it to
be scientifically provable, mathematically demonstrable, that
as a nation, that is, that taking the nation as a whole, we
are in an excellent commercial position, and that the great
efficient cause thereof is Free Trade—that One-sided Free
Trade which our Fair Trading friends exclaim against.
Under our system of free imports we get here everything
that the globe produces on the cheapest possible terms.
This advantage no Protectionist nation enjoys. The poor

among us are thus enabled to fight the battle of life on the most favourable terms possible. Our labourers are thus fed, housed, and clothed as cheaply as possible, and are thus enabled to produce more cheaply than any other workers. This has given us an unmistakable advantage in the world's competition, and of that advantage we cannot be deprived except in one way—by other nations becoming also Free Traders. This being so, we need not be anxious, from a purely selfish national point of view, that Protectionist nations should throw off the fetters which now cramp their energies, but should calmly await the time when the scales shall fall from their eyes. That time may come sooner than some of us expect.

CASSELL, PETTER, GALPIN & CO., BELLE SAUVAGE WORKS, LONDON F.C

www.ingramcontent.com/pod-product-compliance
Lightning Source LLC
Chambersburg PA
CBHW032143080426
42733CB00008B/1189